Unit 1 | Europe Comes to America (1492–1620)

HISTORY & GEOGRAPHY 8
Europe Comes to America (1492–1620)

INTRODUCTION |3

1. QUEST AND CONQUEST 5

EUROPE AWAKENS |6
THE VOYAGES OF COLUMBUS |9
SPANISH CLAIMS AND CONQUESTS |14
SELF TEST 1 |19

2. THE CHASE 21

ENGLISH EFFORTS |22
ENGLAND AND THE NETHERLANDS |25
FRENCH EXPLORATION |26
SELF TEST 2 |32

3. THE FIRST COLONIES 35

SPANISH |36
FRENCH AND DUTCH |37
ENGLISH |40
SELF TEST 3 |48

LIFEPAC Test is located at the back of the booklet. Please remove before starting the unit.

Europe Comes to America (1492–1620) | Unit 1

Author:
Theresa Buskey, B.A., J.D.

Editor:
Alan Christopherson, M.S.

Westover Studios Design Team:
Phillip Pettet, Creative Lead
Teresa Davis, DTP Lead
Nick Castro
Andi Graham
Jerry Wingo

804 N. 2nd Ave. E.
Rock Rapids, IA 51246-1759

© MCMXCIX by Alpha Omega Publications, Inc. All rights reserved.
LIFEPAC is a registered trademark of Alpha Omega Publications, Inc.

All trademarks and/or service marks referenced in this material are the property of their respective owners. Alpha Omega Publications, Inc. makes no claim of ownership to any trademarks and/or service marks other than their own and their affiliates, and makes no claim of affiliation to any companies whose trademarks may be listed in this material, other than their own.

Unit 1 | **Europe Comes to America (1492–1620)**

Europe Comes to America (1492–1620)

Introduction

Man first began to explore and occupy this planet after the division of the languages at Babel (Genesis 11:1-9). Waves of immigrants spread out in all directions and continued to spread for generations as wars and the need for land drove them further. North America was eventually discovered by Asian people who crossed the Bering Strait from Russia thousands of years ago. They migrated south, leaving some settlers in each new place, adapting to each new area as they progressed.

However, the cultural history of the United States did not come from the Native American Peoples who were the first occupants of the land. Instead, the character, languages, customs, history, and philosophy of our country came almost exclusively from the second major wave of immigration. That group came from Europe, beginning in about 1500.

Even though the migration after Babel had spread mankind all over the world, no one knew much about the world as a whole in the 1400s. It was the curious, adventurous, and mostly greedy Europeans who eventually explored and mapped the planet. They did this during the Age of Exploration beginning in the 1400s and continuing through the 1700s. Because of this, much of the history of the world is told from a European perspective. It was the Europeans who made it *world* history. This is especially true for the United States of America.

The history of America must begin in Europe. Many of the people in this country trace their lineage back to the countries of that continent. The language and culture that we all share, no matter what our origins, came from there as well. Our primary religion, Christianity, is the religion of Europe. Europe was the dominant force in the formation of this country and its culture. It is, therefore, where this LIFEPAC® begins the story of America.

Objectives

Read these objectives. The objectives tell you what you will be able to do when you have successfully completed this LIFEPAC. When you have finished this LIFEPAC, you should be able to:

1. Describe the events in the Old World which brought the rebirth of trade.
2. Explain the part Prince Henry played in beginning exploration and match his explorers with their discoveries.
3. Describe the theories and explorations of Columbus.
4. Match Spanish, English, French, and Dutch explorers with their discoveries.
5. Describe the European colonies established in America.

Europe Comes to America (1492–1620) | Unit 1

Survey the LIFEPAC. Ask yourself some questions about this study and write your questions here.

1. QUEST AND CONQUEST

The United States is part of what is called *Western Civilization,* the people and cultures that originated in Western Europe. These people share a Greco-Roman, Judeo-Christian culture. Their history is rooted in the ancient Greek culture as it was absorbed and adapted by the Roman Empire which fell in about AD 500. The philosophy and ideas of those two pagan cultures were changed by the religion of Christianity which itself came out of the Jewish culture. The nations of Western Civilization all share ties to these four cultural ancestors. The history of our particular country starts at the point Western Civilization began its exploration of the world, the exploration that led to the settlement of America.

SECTION OBJECTIVES

Review these objectives. When you have completed this section, you should be able to:

1. Describe the events in the Old World which brought the rebirth of trade.
2. Explain the part Prince Henry played in beginning exploration, and match his explorers with their discoveries.
3. Describe the theories and explorations of Columbus.
4. Match Spanish explorers with their discoveries.
5. Describe the European colonies established in America.

VOCABULARY

Study these words to enhance your learning success in this section.

anarchy (an' är kē). The absence of a system of government and law.

circumnavigate (sėr' kum nav' e gāt). To sail around.

institution (in' stu tü' shun). A club, society, or any organization established for some special purpose.

monopoly (mu nop' u lē). Complete control of an article or service.

viceroy (vīs' roi). A person who rules a country or province, acting as the king's or queen's representative.

Note: *All vocabulary words in this LIFEPAC appear in* **boldface** *print the first time they are used. If you are not sure of the meaning when you are reading, study the definitions given.*

Pronunciation Key: h**a**t, **ā**ge, c**ã**re, f**ä**r; l**e**t, **ē**qual, t**ė**rm; **i**t, **ī**ce; h**o**t, **ō**pen, **ô**rder; **oi**l; **ou**t; c**u**p, p**ů**t, r**ü**le; **ch**ild; lo**ng**; **th**in; /ᵺH/ for **th**en; /zh/ for mea**s**ure; /u/ or /ə/ represents /a/ in **a**bout, /e/ in tak**e**n, /i/ in penc**i**l, /o/ in lem**o**n, and /u/ in circ**u**s.

Europe Awakens

The collapse of the Roman Empire in AD 476 destroyed the central government of Europe. What followed was hundreds of years of **anarchy**, lawlessness, and poverty known as the Medieval Age. Trade was minimal, cities were small, education was rare, and power was in the hands of heavily armed knights who were often little better than thugs. The Roman Catholic Church was the one **institution** that grew during this time. Its influence and power spread as people sought spiritual comfort in a harsh and cruel world. It was a request of the Church that led to the reawakening, the Renaissance, of Europe.

Crusades. In the early AD 1000s, the Holy Land, where Jesus had lived and died, was conquered by a Muslim people known as the Seljuk Turks. They were a threat to the Christian Byzantine Empire of the Middle East and the many Western pilgrims who came to visit Jerusalem each year. The Byzantine emperor asked the Pope, the head of the Catholic Church, for help to defeat the Turks in AD 1095. The Pope made an impassioned appeal to the Catholics of Europe to fight the Muslims and free the Holy Land. Thousands of knights and peasants responded to the call. Thus began the Crusades that would so change Europe.

The Crusades were a series of campaigns occurring over a little more than two hundred years. They were a military failure but a cultural success. The Turks kept the Holy Land, but Europe came into contact with the trade and more advanced scientific knowledge of Asia and North Africa. The Crusaders discovered spices, silk, perfume, and other luxuries from the Far East (China and India) in the markets of the Holy Land. They took these home, and the samples quickly encouraged a demand for more. Spices which preserved and flavored the European diet were especially coveted.

| A Medieval Crusader

Due to the Crusades, trade between Europe and Asia began to grow, as did Europe's knowledge of ancient philosophy, mathematics, astronomy, and geography. The increasing trade and knowledge led to better ships and improved education. Cities grew around markets, and government power expanded to protect trade profits. Moreover, the Crusades sparked the curiosity of Europe about the rest of the world. That spark was fanned into a flame by the travels of Marco Polo in the 1200s.

Marco Polo. Marco Polo was raised as a merchant in Venice, Italy. He left in 1271 at the age of seventeen to travel to China with his father and uncle. It was a difficult, dangerous journey that took three years. When they arrived, they were graciously welcomed by the Chinese emperor, Kublai Khan, who had met Marco's father on an earlier trip.

Unit 1 | **Europe Comes to America (1492–1620)**

The Polos stayed in China for twenty years. Marco gained the emperor's confidence and was sent on many imperial missions within the country. He had ample opportunities to observe the beauty, riches, power, and organization of the Chinese Empire. He learned about gunpowder, printing, coal, and paper money, all of which were unknown in Europe.

The Polos returned to Europe in 1295. The emperor sent them back laden with riches from his country. The porcelain, silk, ivory, jewels, and other luxuries confirmed their stories about the wealth of the eastern lands. In 1298, Marco finished and published a book about his travels. His book, called *Description of the World*, was copied and read all over Europe.

Marco Polo's book was probably one of the most influential non-religious books in history. The riches he described lured the adventurers of Europe. The demand for eastern goods and the curiosity about far away places influenced the Europeans to begin other explorations of their own. The increasingly powerful governments of Europe began to sponsor expeditions to map the world and establish trade. Europe was poised to discover the world.

Answer these questions.

1.1 What are the four cultural ancestors of Western Civilization?

a. _____ b. _____

c. _____ d. _____

1.2 Where did the first occupants of North America come from?

_____

1.3 What two major events caused Europeans to become interested in the Far East?

a. _____ b. _____

1.4 How did the Crusades change Europe?

_____

_____

Complete these sentences.

1.5 The fall of the Roman Empire in the year _____ was followed by a time of anarchy called the _____ Age.

1.6 The one institution that grew in power in the centuries after the fall of Rome was the _____ .

1.7 The Holy Land was captured by the _____ in about 1000.

1.8 Marco Polo visited _____ in the late 1200s.

Section 1 | **7**

Europe Comes to America (1492–1620) | Unit 1

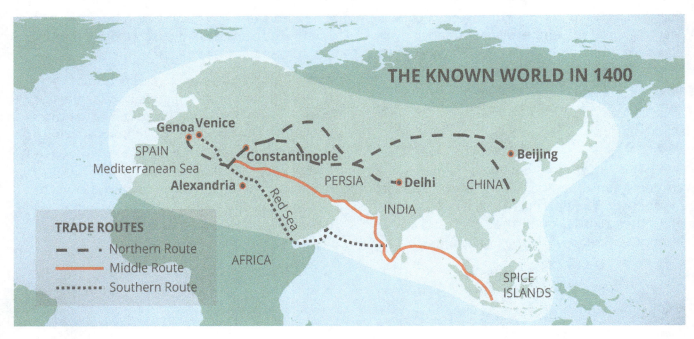

| Overland Trade Routes to Asia; the Known World is highlighted.

The spices and goods of the Far East brought in rich profits for the merchants of Europe as the trade grew into the 1400s. However, there were several problems. The trade between Europe and the Far East was difficult and expensive. Goods had to travel long routes over both land and sea. The land on the trade routes was controlled by Muslims who charged high tolls for safe crossing. Moreover, all the trade converged in the Italian cities on the Mediterranean Sea. These cities had a **monopoly** on the eastern trade that the northern countries deeply resented.

Many of the nations of Europe were becoming better organized and more powerful by the 1400s. These nations, including Portugal, Spain, France, England, and the Netherlands, wanted their own secure trade routes to the Far East. However, they were inhibited by how little they knew about the world. Europeans knew only of Europe, North Africa and southern Asia in the 1400s. Superstition and fear prohibited their gaining knowledge about the rest of the world.

Henry the Navigator (1394-1460). Prince Henry the Navigator was a younger son of King John I of Portugal. He was an excellent organizer with a strong interest in mathematics and astronomy, the sciences of navigation. In 1415 Henry was among the leaders of a Portuguese army that captured the town of Ceuta in North Africa. This brought him into contact with the trade in gold and salt across the Sahara Desert. Henry became interested in discovering the source of the gold down the unknown African coast. He also realized he might be able to find a way to Asia around Africa, cutting off both the Italian cities and the Muslim middlemen in trading with the Far East.

In 1419, Henry became the governor of the southernmost province of Portugal. He began to gather the best navigators, shipbuilders, mapmakers, instrument designers and sailors in Europe. Then, using their skills, he sponsored voyages along the coast of Africa. Each ship was encouraged to sail further than the one before it. By the time of Henry's death in 1460, they had reached as far south as modern-day Sierra Leone. Henry himself never went on the trips, but his work increased Europe's knowledge of navigation, ship building and geography.

Portugal continued Henry's program after his death. The ships brought back gold and slaves which made the voyages profitable. In 1488 a Portuguese captain by the name of Bartholomeu Diaz sailed around the Cape of Good Hope on the southern end of Africa. Ten years later, Vasco da Gama succeeded in sailing a fleet around Africa to India and back. This brought Portugal a secure, direct trade route with the Far East. The monopoly of the Italian cities was broken, the price of eastern goods declined, and Portugal reaped a huge profit that other countries envied and tried to duplicate.

Answer these questions.

1.9 What were three major problems with the Far Eastern trade in the 1400s?

a. _____

b. _____

c. _____

1.10 What two things did Henry the Navigator hope to accomplish by sailing along the coast of Africa?

a. _____

b. _____

Write true if the statement is true. If it is false, write false and change one or two words to make it true.

1.11 _____ Henry the Navigator was a prince of Spain.

1.12 _____ By the time of Henry's death, his ships had reached as far south as modern day Sierra Leone.

1.13 _____ Henry increased Europe's knowledge of navigation, ship building and alchemy.

1.14 _____ Bartholomeu Diaz sailed around Cape of Good Hope in 1488.

1.15 _____ Bartholomeu Diaz sailed a fleet around Africa to India and back in 1498.

1.16 _____ The Portuguese route around Africa broke the Italian monopoly on the Far Eastern trade.

The Voyages of Columbus

For many generations, Spain had been a divided land, split between several Catholic and Muslim nations. The Catholic nations had been slowly uniting, and by the end of the 1400s the final two, Aragon and Castile, had become one by a marriage between their monarchs. The two, Ferdinand and Isabella, united their armies and conquered the last of the Muslim strongholds in Spain. The monarchs were then free to contend with their Iberian rival, Portugal, for trade with the east. Since Portugal had almost completed its route around Africa, Spain turned to an alternative offered by an Italian sailor named Christopher Columbus.

Christopher Columbus (whose name means "Christ bearer") was born in Genoa, Italy in 1451. He was an ambitious, experienced sailor with an innovative idea. The educated people of his day knew the world was round. It had been proven by the ancient Greeks, and Columbus wanted to take advantage of this. He proposed to reach the Indies (the islands south of China) by sailing west from Europe. The problem was that he underestimated the size of the earth by about 25%, and he thought Asia extended further east than it really does. However, he had ambition, foresight, persistence, and a belief that God had chosen him to fulfill this dream.

Columbus had been interested in sailing from an early age. Genoa was a bustling Mediterranean seaport with plenty of opportunities for a young man to learn seafaring skills. Columbus also learned to read and write Latin, the language of educated Europe. He became a sailor in his early adult years. He also worked for a time at his brother's shop in Lisbon, Portugal selling charts and navigational instruments. Portugal was, at the time, opening the trade route around Africa and was the leading European nation in the navigational arts.

When Columbus sought aid to test his idea of sailing west to the Indies, he naturally applied to the king of Portugal. Columbus' estimate of the distance between Europe and Asia was disputed by many experts. The experts were correct; Columbus underestimated the distance by more than half! Yet, it was his stubborn belief in the accuracy of his figures that led to propose his alternative. The king of Portugal, however, believed the experts and was unwilling to accept the extravagant demands Columbus made for himself. The enterprise was refused in 1482.

Columbus tried to interest the rulers of England and France, but both declined. He then petitioned the joint monarchs of Spain, Isabella and Ferdinand. Isabella was interested but was unwilling to pursue the expedition while her

| Christopher Columbus

country was engaged in a war to reconquer Muslim lands in Spain. She set up a team of experts to study the idea.

The last Muslim stronghold in Spain, Granada, was captured in 1492. After Columbus' friends at court used their influence on his behalf, the Spanish monarchs finally agreed to finance his voyage. He was given what he demanded, the title of Admiral, the right to govern the lands he found, and one-tenth of any riches he brought back.

Columbus set sail on August 3, 1492, with three small ships, the *Niña*, the *Pinta*, and the *Santa Maria* with ninety men. The trip was frightening for the superstitious sailors who had never been out of sight of land for so long. It was five long weeks after they left the Canary Islands off Africa until an island was sighted on October 12, 1492. Columbus landed and claimed the island for Spain, calling it San Salvador.

Unit 1 | **Europe Comes to America (1492–1620)**

| The *Niña*, *Pinta*, and *Santa Maria*

Complete these sentences.

1.17 Christopher Columbus was born in _____ , Italy.

1.18 Columbus proposed to reach the Far East by sailing _____ from Europe.

1.19 Columbus underestimated the distance between Europe and Asia by more than _____ .

1.20 Columbus' proposal was rejected by _____ , _____ , and _____ , before it was accepted by Spain.

1.21 _____ and _____ were the Spanish monarchs who sponsored Columbus.

1.22 Spain sponsored Columbus after their army captured the last _____ stronghold of _____ in 1492.

1.23 Columbus' three ships were the _____ , the _____ , and the _____ .

Europe Comes to America (1492–1620) | Unit 1

 Answer this question.

1.24 Why did the king of Portugal reject Columbus' proposal?

_____

_____

Columbus was convinced that he was in the islands of the Indies. He even called the Indigenous people "Indians," a name that stuck even after the mistake was discovered. The islands of the Caribbean where he landed were eventually named the West Indies to distinguish them from the East Indies of Asia.

Columbus spent about three months exploring the beautiful islands. He found only virgin lands, small villages, and a few gold trinkets. The *Santa Maria* was wrecked on the island of Hispaniola in December. This convinced Columbus that it was time to return and report what he had found. He captured a few of the natives and obtained some gold to take with him. Thirty-eight men were left behind on Hispaniola to search for more gold until his return. They were housed in a fort made from the lumber of the *Santa Maria*.

Columbus returned safely to Spain in March of 1493 to a hero's welcome. The king and queen greeted him with great honor when he arrived at court. He was confirmed in the privileges he had been promised and plans were made for another voyage. The Spanish monarchs wanted to secure their claim on these islands which they hoped to use as a base for trade with Asia.

Later Voyages. Columbus sailed again in September of 1493 with 17 ships and over a thousand men. Most were going to get rich quick, but a few were priests sent to convert the Native Americans. The men Columbus had left behind were all dead by the time he arrived. They were probably killed by the Native Americans, whom the explorers had mistreated. Columbus established a new settlement on Hispaniola, named La Isabela, the first successful European colony in America.

Problems quickly began to develop. Columbus was unable to find the mainland of China or the islands of Japan which he expected were nearby. The colonists did not find instant riches and began to resent Columbus' autocratic ways. The peaceful Native Americans rebelled against the Spanish attempts to enslave them and force them to find gold. Despite this, Columbus returned to Spain and secured the continued support of the monarchs.

During his third voyage, in 1498, Columbus reached the coast of Central America, but still did not find the great cities he was expecting. In the meantime, complaints about his management of the Spanish colonies reached the ears of the king and queen of Spain. They sent a commissioner to investigate. The officer arrested Columbus and his brother and sent them back to Spain in chains. The king and queen ordered him freed as soon as the story of his arrest reached them. However, they were now unwilling to allow Columbus to govern the new lands. He was permitted to return in another attempt to locate China.

Columbus left on his last voyage in May of 1502. He was forbidden to land at Hispaniola except if he needed supplies. He explored the coast of Honduras, Costa Rica, Nicaragua and Panama looking for passage through these lands to China. He was forced to abandon his ships after they became unseaworthy. He and his crew were marooned for a year on the island of Jamaica waiting for help. Finally, ships were sent to rescue him, and he arrived safely back in Spain in November of 1504.

Columbus died less than two years later, a disappointed and bitter man. The king (Isabella had died) refused to restore his authority over the lands he had discovered. Many other people were now exploring and settling the lands he felt belonged to him. He did not even receive the honor of having the new continents named after him. That accolade went to Amerigo Vespucci who was a part of explorations of the "New World" beginning in 1497. (The editor of a geography book in 1507 suggested the name America, believing Vespucci had discovered it, and the name stuck). Columbus, on the other hand, died still believing he had found a new route to the Far East. He was a failure in one sense. He had not found a way to Asia and he had lost control of what he did find. Columbus was certainly one of the most successful failures in the history of mankind.

We also know now that Columbus was not the first European to reach America. That honor goes to Viking explorers under the leadership of Leif Ericson. The Vikings of Greenland (a part of Denmark) tried to start a colony in Newfoundland, Canada about the year AD 1000.

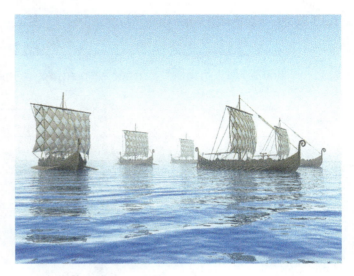

| Viking Ships

The colony failed and Europe never became aware of the continent's existence. It was Columbus' failed attempt to reach Asia that led to permanent contact between Europe and the Americas. Therefore, as far as Western Civilization is concerned, Columbus *did* discover America.

Answer these questions.

1.25 Where was the first successful European colony founded and by whom?

a. _____

b. _____

1.26 How many voyages did Columbus make to America? _____

1.27 Did Columbus ever reach the continent of North America? (Check your facts carefully.)

_____

1.28 Who were the continents of the New World named after?

_____

1.29 What did Columbus wrongly believe until his death about the lands he had discovered?

_____

Europe Comes to America (1492–1620) | Unit 1

1.30 Who were the very first Europeans to reach America?

_____

1.31 Why was Columbus' contact with America significant?

_____

_____

Spanish Claims and Conquests

It gradually became apparent to the explorers that this was a "New World," not Asia. Some saw it as a large obstacle between them and the riches of the Far East. Others saw it as an undeveloped land of potentially great wealth. For years afterward the explorers sought to get around it, claim part of it or both.

Spain had a significant head start over the rest of Europe in the New World. Few other countries were secure enough at home to risk expensive voyages of discovery. The only immediate rival was Portugal, which was busy exploiting its trade around Africa. The two leading maritime nations quickly agreed to divide the yet unmapped lands "fairly."

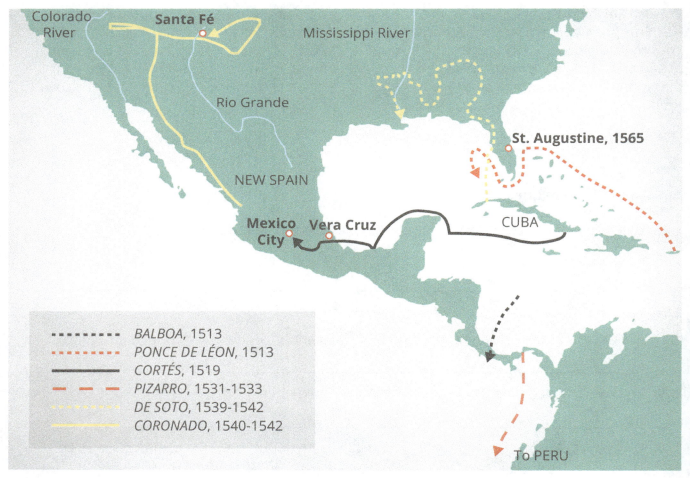

| Routes of the Conquistadors

Unit 1 | **Europe Comes to America (1492–1620)**

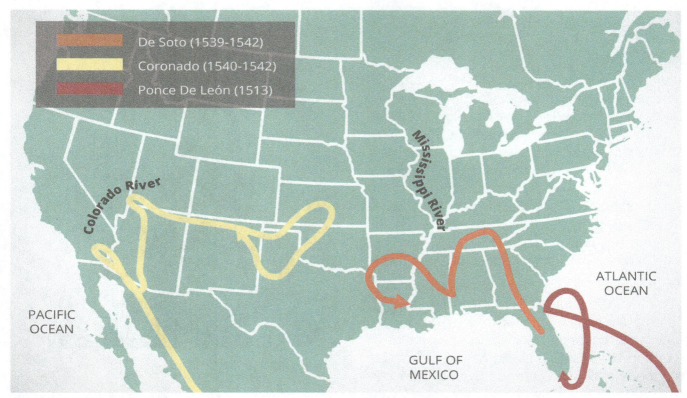

| Spanish Explorations in North America

According to the terms of the Treaty of Tordesillas in 1494, the non-Christian lands were divided between the two nations by a line (called the Line of Demarcation) that ran through the North Atlantic and cut Brazil in two. (The treaty moved a line set up by the Pope a year earlier). Portugal took everything east of the line, including Africa, the East Indies, and Brazil. Spain took everything west of the line, including all of North America and most of South America! Of course, such huge claims proved impossible to enforce when the other nations began to explore and colonize.

Columbus' discoveries generated great excitement in Spain. Many poor noblemen and soldiers who were out of work now that the Muslims were defeated looked to the new lands as a way to gain wealth and fame. Hundreds of Spanish *conquistadors* (conquerors) came with the express purpose of taking over Native American lands and finding gold to make themselves rich.

In the process of searching for treasure, they also explored and mapped the land, though that was not their purpose.

Balboa. Nunez de Balboa was a well born man who came to the New World in 1501. He helped found a settlement on the Isthmus of Panama. From that base he led an expedition across the Isthmus in 1513. He was the first European to cross the Isthmus and see the Pacific Ocean on the other side. He claimed all of the land touching the ocean for Spain and began a settlement to allow future conquests. The ocean he found was one indication that eventually led the Spaniards to conclude that they had not yet reached Asia.

Ponce de León. Juan Ponce de León was a Spanish nobleman who came to the New World on Columbus' second voyage. He was a soldier who conquered the island of Puerto Rico and became its governor in 1509. After losing that post, he received permission to search the nearby land for the "Fountain of Youth."

European legends said that it was the water of life from the Garden of Eden which was supposed to be in the Far East.

Ponce de León led an expedition that landed on a peninsula north of the West Indies in 1513. De León arrived during "Pascua Florida," (Spanish for "Flowery Easter," referring to the Easter season) and saw the area's beautiful flowers. He claimed the land for Spain and named it *Florida* which means *flowery* in Spanish. He explored much of the coastline of the state, but never found the Fountain of Youth. He led an attempt to colonize the land in 1521, but the local Native American people drove him away.

Magellan. Ferdinand Magellan was an explorer, not a conquistador. He was a Portuguese sea captain who set out with five ships under Spanish sponsorship to **circumnavigate** the world in 1519. Spain still did not know how big the lands of the New World were or how close they were to Asia. Magellan believed they were very close, and a trip around South America would be an easy route to Asia.

Magellan sailed south along the coast of South America searching for a way around the continent. He sailed into every river mouth and tasted the water. If it was fresh, he knew it did not connect to the ocean. Finally, almost a year after leaving Spain, he found the strait that now bears his name at the southern tip of South America. He sailed through the dangerous passage into the calm waters of the ocean he named the "Pacific," which means peaceful.

Magellan believed this was a small ocean and Asia was only a short distance away. The three remaining ships sailed for almost a hundred days without seeing any inhabited land. The wretched men ate rats and leather to avoid starvation. Many died anyway. The ships eventually reached the Philippines where Magellan was killed. Two ships reached the Spice Islands and took on cargo for the voyage home. One ship, the *Victoria*, made it safely back to Spain around Africa in September of 1522 with eighteen men aboard.

| A Conquistador

The route Magellan had scouted was too long and dangerous for a regular trade route. However, his voyage, one of the greatest in human history, proved the world was a sphere and that the New World was a long way from Asia. However, for many years, men would continue to search for a water route through the Americas or around them to the north. The lure of the Far East was not so easily ignored.

Cortes and Pizarro. Two of the most infamous conquistadors had only an indirect effect on the United States. Hernando Cortes conquered the fabulously wealthy Aztec of central Mexico in 1519-1521. Francisco Pizarro ruthlessly did the same to the gold- and silver-rich Inca civilization of Peru in 1532. These conquests brought unimaginable wealth to Spain and two important results for America. First, Spain began to concentrate its attention and control on these lands of proven wealth, leaving the northern lands sparsely occupied. Second, the sudden wealth excited the interest and greed of the other nations of Europe who began to stake their own claims in the New World.

De Soto. Hernando de Soto came to the New World as a teenager and was a part of Pizzaro's conquest of the Incas. He became very wealthy in his post as lieutenant governor of Cusco, the Inca capital. Greedy for more wealth, he led an expedition through northern Florida and Mississippi searching for gold in 1539.

De Soto and his men were the first Europeans to discover the Mississippi River. They explored parts of what are now Georgia, Alabama, Mississippi, and Arkansas, searching for gold and fighting Native Americans. De Soto died of a fever in 1542. The expedition continued without him and continued as far west as Texas before returning safely to a Spanish settlement on the Gulf of Mexico.

Coronado. Francisco Coronado was a Spanish nobleman without a family fortune who came to Mexico in 1538 with the **viceroy** of New Galica (northwest of Mexico City). The viceroy heard rumors of seven cities of gold north of his province. He commissioned Coronado to find the cities and conquer them for Spain.

Coronado set out in 1540 from Mexico and went into the area that is now the southwest United States. He and his men never did find the golden cities, but they did explore parts of Arizona, New Mexico, Texas, and Kansas. Breaking off into smaller groups, the Spaniards were the first Europeans to see the Grand Canyon, the Rio Grande Valley, and Palo Duro Canyon in Texas. They also discovered the pueblo towns made by the Indigenous people of the Southwest. They finally returned, empty handed, in 1542.

Results. The explorations of Ponce de León, de Soto and Coronado proved to be a disappointment for Spain. After the riches of Mexico and Peru, the northern lands seemed to be poor pickings. The explorations did, however, give Spain a claim to much of the southern United States to add to their huge American empire. That empire stretched from Arizona to the Straits of Magellan. The gold and riches gathered from this vast land made Spain the richest and most powerful European nation of its time. Columbus' mistake had paid off handsomely.

 Name the man in each of these descriptions.

1.32 _____ explored and named Florida

1.33 _____ first European to cross the Isthmus of Panama

1.34 _____ searched in North America for the Fountain of Youth

1.35 _____ led the first successful circumnavigation of the world

1.36 _____ explored Arizona, New Mexico and Texas

1.37 _____ conquered the Inca

1.38 _____ his voyage proved the New World was not part of Asia

1.39 _____ first European to find the Mississippi River

1.40 _____ conquered the Aztec

1.41 _____ explored the southwest U.S. looking for cities of gold

1.42 _____ explored Mississippi, Georgia, Arkansas and Alabama

Answer these questions about the Treaty of Tordesillas.

1.43 Which two nations signed the treaty?
_____

1.44 What was the purpose of the treaty?
_____
_____

1.45 What was the line created by the treaty called?
_____

Answer these questions.

1.46 Who were the conquistadors and what did they accomplish for Spain?
_____
_____
_____

1.47 What two things did Magellan's voyage prove?

a. _____

b. _____

1.48 What two effects did the conquests of Cortes and Pizarro have on U.S. history?

a. _____

b. _____

Write a one-page paper on one of the following topics.

1.49 Leif Ericson and the first European settlement in America
The Crusades
Kublai Khan and his empire
Ferdinand and Isabella of Spain
Navigation in the 1400 and 1500s
The Inca Empire
The Aztec Empire

TEACHER CHECK _____ _____
　　　　　　　　　　　　initials　　date

Review the material in this section in preparation for the Self Test. The Self Test will check your mastery of this particular section. The items missed on this Self Test will indicate specific areas where restudy is needed for mastery.

SELF TEST 1

Match the following (each answer, 3 points).

1.01	_____ first to cross the Isthmus of Panama	a.	Hernando de Soto
1.02	_____ explored Florida searching for the Fountain of Youth	b.	Francisco Coronado
		c.	Francisco Pizarro
1.03	_____ led the first circumnavigation of the world	d.	Nunez de Balboa
1.04	_____ led a fleet to Asia around Africa and back again	e.	Ponce de León
1.05	_____ conquered the Inca	f.	Vasco da Gama
1.06	_____ conquered the Aztec	g.	Hernando Cortes
1.07	_____ lived in China in the 1200s and wrote a famous book about it	h.	Leif Ericson
		i.	Marco Polo
1.08	_____ Viking leader of the first Europeans in America	j.	Ferdinand Magellan
1.09	_____ explored the American southwest looking for cities of gold		
1.010	_____ first to see the Mississippi River		

Answer these questions (each answer, 4 points).

1.011 What was the Treaty of Tordesillas and what did it do?

_____

_____

_____

1.012 What were the Crusades and what effect did they have on Europe?

_____

_____

_____

1.013 What were the major problems in trading with the Far East in 1400?

_____

_____

_____

Europe Comes to America (1492–1620) | Unit 1

1.014 Who was Henry the Navigator and what did he accomplish?

_____

_____

_____

1.015 What are the four cultural ancestors of Western Civilization?

a. _____   b. _____

c. _____   d. _____

Check the statements that are true of Christopher Columbus (each answer, 3 points).

1.016 _____ He was very ambitious, claiming great rewards for his work.

1.017 _____ He thought the world was smaller than it really is.

1.018 _____ He knew he had discovered an unknown land between Europe and Asia.

1.019 _____ He was a well-educated Italian sailor from Genoa.

1.020 _____ Portugal was also interested in sponsoring him.

1.021 _____ He was the only person who believed the world was round.

1.022 _____ Ferdinand and Isabella agreed to the voyage only after the defeat of Granada.

1.023 _____ His ships were the *Victoria*, the *Santa Maria*, and the *Hispaniola*.

1.024 _____ He established the first successful European settlement in America.

1.025 _____ He never landed in North America.

1.026 _____ He made four voyages to the New World.

1.027 _____ He named the new continents after his son, Amerigo.

1.028 _____ He died a happy man, rich in honors and power.

1.029 _____ At one point, he was sent back to Spain in chains.

Answer true or false (each answer, 2 points).

1.030 _____ Columbus' mistake was good for Spain.

1.031 _____ The very first occupants of the Americas came by boat from Africa.

1.032 _____ The United States is part of Western Civilization.

1.033 _____ The Europeans of 1400 knew only about Europe, North Africa, and part of Asia.

80 / 100   SCORE _____   TEACHER _____ _____
                                                initials   date

2. THE CHASE

Spain had a substantial head start on claiming and colonizing the New World. By the middle of the 1500s, Spain had about two hundred settlements and over 100,000 settlers in the Americas. The tremendous wealth Spain accumulated, especially from Mexico and Peru, tempted even the most cautious monarchs of Europe. Other countries began to send expeditions to claim land and, presumably, riches. Three nations: England, the Netherlands, and France sent explorers, and later settlers, to secure some of the booty in the future United States. This section will discuss these explorers and the lands they claimed for their countries.

| Columbus, Queen Isabella, and King Ferdinand

SECTION OBJECTIVES

Review these objectives. When you have completed this section, you should be able to:

4. Match Spanish, English, French, and Dutch explorers with their discoveries.
5. Describe the European colonies established in America.

VOCABULARY

Study these words to enhance your learning success in this section.

advocate (ad' vu kit). A person who speaks in favor of something; supporter.

implacable (im' plak u bul). Not capable of being appeased; significantly changed or mitigated.

Jesuit (jez' u wit). A member of the Roman Catholic Society of Jesus founded by Ignatius Loyola in 1534 and devoted to missionary and educational work.

mutiny (myüt' n ē). An open rebelling against lawful authority, especially by sailors or soldiers against their officers.

portage (pôr' tij). A carrying of boats or provisions overland from one river or lake to another.

privateer (prī' vu tir'). An armed private ship commissioned to sail against the trade or warships of an enemy.

seasonal (sē' zn ul). Occurring at a particular season; happening at regular intervals.

succession (suk sesh' un). The order or arrangement of persons having the right to succeed to an office, property, or rank.

English Efforts

The king of England at the time Columbus sailed was Henry VII of the Tudor dynasty. England had just come through a long civil war, The War of the Roses. Henry had become king by success in battle and legitimized his conquest by marrying the heiress of the opposing family. Henry was too busy securing his own position to waste much money or effort on speculative voyages. However, there came a time when even he realized the potential importance and wealth of a new route to the Indies.

John Cabot. John Cabot was an Italian sailor and merchant who came to live in England by 1480. He heard of Columbus' voyages and sought to secure a trade route to Asia for himself and England. In 1496 he received authorization from King Henry to search for unknown lands and received a monopoly on the trade he established. In turn, the king was to receive one-fifth of the profits. Henry did not finance the voyage, however. The merchants from the city of Bristol had to pay for the voyage.

Cabot sailed in May of 1497 from Bristol on one small ship, the *Matthew*, with a crew of eighteen men. He took a more northerly route than Columbus, sailing west from Ireland. He made landfall on June 24 in what is now Canada. The exact spot where he landed is not known for certain, but it was most likely in the area of Newfoundland or Cape Breton Island. He claimed the land for the king of England.

John Cabot was also convinced that he had reached Asia even though he did not find the wealthy cities of China and the Indies. What he did find was the Grand Banks, one of the finest fishing grounds in the world, just off the coast of Canada. He also gave England a claim to land in North America.

Cabot returned to England in August to report his discoveries. Believing he had found a route to Asia, Henry VII made him an admiral and granted him a pension. John Cabot set off again in 1498 on another larger expedition, the

| John Cabot's Ship

outcome of which is uncertain. It is possible, however, that Cabot or his son explored the coast of North America as far south as Virginia, giving England a large land claim in the New World.

The discovery of the Grand Banks had an immediate effect. England was dependent upon fish from Iceland. The English fishermen moved quickly to exploit this area that was so rich in fish that, according to Cabot, they could be scooped up in a basket. However, it would be over a hundred years before England would take advantage of Cabot's other discoveries and begin colonies in the New World.

Interim. England was too busy with difficulties in Europe to pursue developing its North American claims. Henry VIII, son of Henry VII, prompted a major religious conflict by taking England out of the Catholic church and by marrying six different women in order to have sons to secure the **succession**. He was followed on the throne by his son Edward VI, who died young. The next ruler was Henry's daughter, Mary I, who became known as "Bloody Mary" for her violent attempts to re-establish Catholicism in England. Finally, in 1558, Henry VIII's last child, Elizabeth I, came to the throne.

The long reign of this clever, careful woman laid the foundation for English expansion all over the globe.

Sea Dogs. Spain and England were bitter enemies during most of Elizabeth's reign, and Spain controlled much of the New World. Lacking the resources to develop their own colonies in America, many of the other countries took to raiding Spanish ports and vessels. These pirates worked out of the many hidden harbors of the Caribbean Islands near the Spanish possessions. Elizabeth I actively supported English pirates, called sea dogs, who attacked Spanish towns and trading fleets. The attacks kept the Spanish fleet busy, reduced Spain's profit, and provided income for the queen. When war broke out between Spain and England, the pirates were licensed by the queen as **privateers**.

Francis Drake. The greatest of the sea dogs was Sir Francis Drake. Drake was a skilled sailor, soldier, and organizer. He made several voyages to the West Indies that gained him the reputation of a successful and determined enemy of Spain. He earned his fortune and fame by an attack on a Spanish town in Panama in 1572 under a privateer's license from the queen.

Drake's greatest fame, however, came from a voyage around the world that began in 1577. He sailed from England with five ships, intending to reach the Pacific and loot Spanish ports there. He and the queen also hoped he could find evidence on the west coast of a passage across North America (the Northwest Passage). The search for a way to Asia was still ongoing.

Drake sailed down the coast of South America and around the southern tip into the Pacific Ocean. By that time, he had lost all but one of his ships, which he renamed the *Golden Hind*. He traveled up the west coast of the Americas, attacking Spanish towns and ships. The Spaniards were caught completely off guard. Before that time, no other nation had sent ships into the Pacific. The *Golden Hind* was heavily laden with gold and silver by the time it reached what is now the United States.

Drake explored the west coast as far north as Vancouver, Canada, searching unsuccessfully for the Northwest Passage. During the trip he landed in California, near San Francisco, and claimed the land for England. Eventually, the cold forced him to turn back. Drake had not initially intended to sail around the world, but he did not want to risk sailing back along the Spanish-held coast. So in July of 1579, he instead headed west across the Pacific Ocean toward Asia.

Drake traded for spices in the East Indies and safely sailed around Africa with his one ship and about fifty remaining men. He returned to England in September of 1580, a very wealthy national hero. The king of Spain demanded that he be punished for his attacks on Spanish property. Instead, Queen Elizabeth went on board his ship and made him a knight.

Spain reduced. Spain now launched a full attack on England, intending to conquer that land. The huge Spanish fleet was called the "Invincible Armada." It was destroyed by the smaller English navy (Drake was one of the commanders) and bad weather in 1588. The defeat was just one of several factors that broke the immense power and wealth of Spain. The government had been overspending its American treasure and managing its colonies badly. The repeated attacks of the sea dogs, as well as rebellions in Spanish lands, further sapped the strength of the European giant. By the end of the 1500s, Spain was in decline, and other players from Europe began to seriously exploit the Americas.

Europe Comes to America (1492–1620) | Unit 1

Complete these sentences.

2.1 The ruler of England in 1492 was _____ of the house of Tudor.

2.2 The man whose explorations gave England its first claim to North America was _____ .

2.3 The greatest of the English sea dogs was _____ .

2.4 The English monarch whose long reign laid the foundation for British expansion all over the world was _____ .

2.5 One of John Cabot's discoveries was the rich fishing grounds of the _____ .

2.6 In 1588 Spain sent the so-called _____ to attack and conquer England.

Answer these questions.

2.7 What did John Cabot accomplish for England?
_____
_____
_____

2.8 Why did Elizabeth I support the English pirates in the Caribbean?
_____
_____
_____

2.9 What did Sir Francis Drake accomplish on his trip around the world?
_____
_____
_____

2.10 What caused the decline of Spanish power at the end of the 1500s?
_____
_____
_____

England and the Netherlands

An English explorer named Henry Hudson provided both England and the Netherlands with claims in the New World. Virtually nothing is known about Henry Hudson before he went on four voyages to explore the Arctic beginning in 1607. He was searching for a northern route to Asia. Drake and Magellan had established that the route south of the continents was simply too long to be commercially usable. Merchants in Europe still desperately wanted a direct route to the Indies.

Hudson sailed from England in 1607 on a small ship called the *Hopewell*. The voyage was sponsored by the Muscovy Company which was hoping to find a route around the northern side of Europe to Asia (the Northeast Passage—north and east of Europe). Hudson sailed north to the polar ice pack and then east along it. He was forced to return by the huge ice floes that threatened his ship. A second attempt in 1608 was also stopped by ice. The Muscovy Company refused to finance another trip.

Hudson was then hired by the Dutch East India Company from the Netherlands. His assignment was to again try and find a northern route around Europe to Asia. Instead, Hudson was interested in reports of a possible passageway through North America. After leaving the Netherlands in 1609, he convinced his crew to change the mission and they went west instead.

Hudson explored along the east coast of what is now the United States on this first voyage to the New World. He went as far south as North Carolina. He also explored Chesapeake and Delaware Bay looking for a passageway to the Pacific Ocean. He sailed over 100 miles up what is now called the Hudson River in New York, hoping it would lead west. He eventually realized it did not, but he did claim the river and nearby land for the Netherlands. It would turn out to be a rich prize because the Hudson River Valley was fertile and had an abundance of fur animals, with an excellent harbor at the river's mouth.

Hudson tried again in 1610 to find the Northwest Passage to Asia (northwest from Europe) around North America. This time, he was again under English sponsorship. He believed he had succeeded when he sailed through a strait south of Baffin Island, Canada (now called the Hudson Strait) and into a huge body of open water. In fact, he had discovered one of the largest bays in the world, Hudson Bay.

They sailed south along the edge of the Bay looking for the Pacific Ocean. Eventually, Hudson and his men were trapped as the bay froze over in the Canadian cold. The men suffered through a difficult winter. In the spring, Hudson wanted to continue the search, but his crew **mutinied**. Hudson, his son, and a few others were abandoned in a small boat and the ship returned to England. Nothing was ever heard of Hudson or his group again. He had given England a huge claim to the land of Canada, a claim they would soon begin to use.

| Hudson's Explorations

Write true if the statement is true. If it is false, write false and change one or two words to make it true.

2.11 _____ Hudson's two voyages in 1609 and 1610 were in search of the Northeast Passage to Asia.

2.12 _____ Hudson sailed two times for England and two times for the Netherlands.

2.13 _____ Hudson was hired by both the Muscovy Company and the Dutch East India Company.

2.14 _____ Hudson gave the Netherlands their claim to the land around Hudson Bay.

2.15 _____ Hudson was abandoned by his men in Canada after they survived a difficult winter there.

2.16 _____ Hudson's last voyage gave England a large claim to parts of what is now the United States.

French Exploration

In the scramble for American land, the French succeeded in securing a large part of what is now south and eastern Canada and the central United States for themselves. These claims were based on the work of many different explorers. The French came in through the St. Lawrence River and spread out to the south along the Great Lakes and the Mississippi River.

France was one of several nations whose fleets came every year to the Grand Banks to fish in the early 1500s. The fishermen set up **seasonal** settlements on shore to dry their fish for shipment back to Europe. The visitors became acquainted with the Gulf of the St. Lawrence and the islands near it, information they passed on to later explorers. The New World wealth captured by Spain eventually attracted the attention of the king of France. In 1534 he commissioned a voyage to explore west of the fishing grounds searching for gold and a passageway to Asia.

Jacques Cartier. The man chosen to lead the French expedition was Jacques Cartier, an accomplished French navigator. He sailed from France in 1534 with two ships and about sixty men. The expedition explored the Gulf of St. Lawrence and went west as far as Anticosti Island near the mouth of the St. Lawrence River. Cartier returned to France with two Native Americans who claimed that gold and jewels could be obtained further west.

Cartier was sent back the next year with three ships and about 100 men. He sailed west through the Gulf of St. Lawrence and on August 10, 1535, the Feast Day of St. Lawrence, he discovered a large river going into the continent. He followed the newly named St. Lawrence River as far as the present day city of Montreal where rapids stopped his ships. He and his men spent the winter back down the river at the present site of Quebec before returning to France.

The harsh, cold winter was a shock to the Frenchmen who were used to the mild climate of western Europe. Nevertheless, the king of France authorized Cartier to establish a colony on the river in 1541 and sent a French nobleman, Roberval, as commander of the project. Cartier explored further west on foot but never found the precious metals he believed were there. He returned to France after surviving another winter at the settlement near modern-day Quebec. The settlement was abandoned in 1543, and the few survivors returned to France. The French now had a claim to most of the St. Lawrence River, its mouth, and the land around them.

Samuel de Champlain. Wars and religious strife restricted French involvement in the New World for the remainder of the 16th century. Finally, early in the 1600s, King Henry IV of France was ready to try again. He turned to Samuel de Champlain to colonize the French lands and to continue to hunt for the elusive Northwest Passage.

Champlain was an experienced French navigator and soldier. He had made several voyages around the turn of the century to the Americas to trade with the Spanish colonies. He had written a book about his travels which brought him to the attention of the king. Beginning in 1603, Champlain made a series of voyages to North America that expanded and solidified French claims.

In 1603 Champlain traced the St. Lawrence to the Great Lakes, exploring extensively. The following year he explored the east coast beginning at the Gulf of the St. Lawrence and going south of Massachusetts Bay. In 1605 he helped found a settlement called Port Royal that did not survive, south of the Gulf of St. Lawrence. Finally, in 1608, after searching extensively for the best site, he established the city of Quebec, the first successful settlement in what was known as New France.

Champlain quickly made friends with the Huron and Algonquin people near his settlement. In 1609 he even joined some of them on a raid against the Iroquois of northern New York. The use of French firearms caused the Iroquois to flee in terror. It also made the well-organized Iroquois Nation into an **implacable** enemy of France. The Iroquois would, in the future, be a major obstacle to French settlement south of Lakes Ontario and Erie, as well as willing English allies in the fight for control of the continent. On this trip, Champlain was the first European to see the large lake in New York that bears his name.

In the following years, Champlain explored the Ottawa River and reached Lake Huron. He made several trips to France on behalf of Quebec. He led the defense of the city when England besieged it in 1628 and was captured in 1629 when Quebec fell. The city was returned to France by a treaty in 1632 and Champlain was released. He returned to rebuild and lived in Quebec until his death in 1635. His many contributions to the development of French colonial interests earned him the title of the "Father of New France."

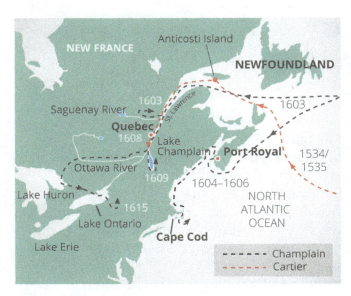

| Cartier's and Champlain's Explorations

Answer these questions.

2.17 Where did the first regular French visitors come to North America and why?
_____
_____

2.18 What area did Jacques Cartier explore?
_____
_____

2.19 What area did Samuel de Champlain explore?
_____
_____
_____

2.20 What was the result of Champlain's attack on the Iroquois?
_____
_____
_____

Answer these questions with yes or no.

2.21 _____ Was Cartier's first mission to search for gold and the Northwest Passage?

2.22 _____ Did Cartier ever establish a successful settlement in America?

2.23 _____ Was the St. Lawrence River named for the captain of the ship that found it?

2.24 _____ Did Cartier earn the title "Father of New France?"

2.25 _____ Had Europeans lost interest in searching for a route to Asia by the early 1600s?

Fur trade. The vital "crop" of New France was fur. Fur was a coveted status symbol in Europe and profits were high. Beaver was especially prized. The demand for furs drew French woodsmen, called *coureurs de bois* ("runners of the woods"), deeper and deeper into the continent. These were generally wild, independent men who worked alone or in small groups, trading and trapping. They were often followed by Catholic priests who tried to convert and protect the Native American people.

Eventually, the *coureurs de bois* set up trading posts and forts to secure their trade routes. The priests set up missions. They were friendly with the Native Americans whom they depended on to supply them with furs and converts. In this way, the French lands were expanded and secured. However, it could not be well secured because the numbers of the French were so few and they were spread out over such a vast area of land.

Jolliet and Marquette. As the French woodsmen spread out in the area of the Great Lakes, they began to hear about a large river to the south. The Native Americans called it *Mississippi*, which meant "big river." Since the French were still hoping to find a waterway to the Pacific and Asia, the governor of New France commissioned an expedition to explore the river. It was led by Louis Jolliet, a *coureurs de bois*, and Jacques Marquette, a **Jesuit** priest. They were instructed to find the large river and follow it to its mouth.

The expedition set off in 1673. Using canoes, they paddled up the Fox River from Lake Michigan in what is now Wisconsin. They **portaged** from the source of the Fox to the nearby Wisconsin River, a tributary of the Mississippi. They followed the river until they reached the Mississippi in June of 1673. They followed the river's course, interviewing the friendly Native American people as they went. Eventually, the information from the Native Americans and the southward direction of the river convinced them that it flowed to the Gulf of Mexico, not the Pacific.

They continued south until they reached the point where the Mississippi was joined by the Arkansas River. There they met hostile Native Americans for the first time. They were also told by others that there were white men further down the river. Certain now that the river went to Spanish territory in the Gulf of Mexico, the explorers turned back. They returned up the Illinois River and portaged to the Chicago River, bringing them back to Lake Michigan. The trip had taken five months and expanded French claims to much of the northern Mississippi.

Sieur de La Salle. Sieur de La Salle was a wealthy landowner and fur trader in New France. He was also a good friend of the governor of New France and a firm **advocate** of expanding the colony. In 1669 he set off from Montreal to explore the land to the south. He too was hoping to find a river that crossed the

| Marquette and Jolliet

continent to the Pacific. He traveled for four years across the unexplored land south of the Great Lakes around the Ohio River. Eventually, he was convinced that the river flowed to the Gulf of Mexico. He returned to Canada in 1673.

In 1677 La Salle obtained permission to explore the Mississippi from the king of France. Several other projects delayed him, but in 1682 he started down the Mississippi, reaching the mouth in April. He claimed the entire area drained by the river for the King Louis of France, naming it Louisiana. That claim covered most of what is now the central United States, from the Rocky Mountains to the Appalachians.

La Salle returned up the river and established a stronghold called Fort St. Louis to secure French claims on the Illinois River. Then, he went to France for permission to secure the mouth of the river. King Louis XIV agreed to La Salle's request. La Salle sailed from France with 300 colonists in 1684. However, he missed the mouth of the Mississippi and landed in Texas instead. He set up the colony there, but it never prospered. He was killed by his own men while leading an expedition north for help. The settlement failed, and without his leadership no immediate attempt was made to secure the mouth of the river against Spanish intrusion.

Europe Comes to America (1492–1620) | Unit 1

Complete these sentences.

2.26 French claims were expanded by independent traders/woodsmen called _____ .

2.27 The most important export for New France was _____ .

2.28 The Native Americans told the French about a large river called the _____ .

2.29 France was still looking for a water passage to the continent of _____ .

2.30 Sienur de La Salle was a wealthy _____ and _____ trader.

2.31 La Salle named the land he claimed for France in 1682 _____ .

Complete these items.

2.32 Describe the area <u>explored</u> by Jolliet and Marquette.

_____
_____
_____
_____
_____
_____
_____

2.33 Describe the area <u>explored</u> by La Salle.

_____
_____
_____
_____
_____
_____
_____

2.34 Describe the area claimed by La Salle for France.

_____
_____
_____
_____
_____
_____

Review the material in this section in preparation for the Self Test. This Self Test will check your mastery of this particular section as well as your knowledge of all previous sections.

Europe Comes to America (1492–1620) | Unit 1

SELF TEST 2

Name the country that sponsored each explorer, then describe the land he <u>explored</u> (2 points for the country, 6 points for the description).

2.01 Jacques Cartier – country
_____
_____
_____

2.02 Henry Hudson (first American voyage) – country
_____
_____
_____

2.03 Henry Hudson (second American voyage) – country
_____
_____
_____

2.04 Samuel de Champlain – country
_____
_____
_____

2.05 John Cabot – country
_____
_____
_____

2.06 Marquette and Jolliet – country
_____
_____
_____

2.07 Sieur de La Salle – country
_____
_____
_____

Match these people with their description (each answer, 3 points).

2.08 _____ Sir Francis Drake
2.09 _____ Iroquois
2.010 _____ Aztec
2.011 _____ Leif Ericson
2.012 _____ Christopher Columbus
2.013 _____ Ferdinand Magellan
2.014 _____ Henry the Navigator
2.015 _____ Ponce de León
2.016 _____ Crusaders
2.017 _____ Marco Polo

a. led the first expedition around the world
b. visited China and wrote about it in 1200s
c. organized voyages around Africa to India
d. wealthy Indigenous people of Mexico
e. Viking leader of first Europeans to land in America
f. fought to defeat Muslims in Holy Land
g. sea dog, went around the world looting Spanish towns and ships
h. Indigenous Nation that originally lived near New York
i. accidentally sailed into the Americas looking for Asia in 1492
j. explored Florida looking for the Fountain of Youth

Answer true or false (each answer, 2 points).

2.018 _____ The French path of exploration went down the St. Lawrence River, across the Great Lakes and down the Mississippi River.

2.019 _____ Spanish power kept other countries out of America until almost 1700.

2.020 _____ New France's most important product was food crops.

2.021 _____ The Grand Banks was a fishing area near Newfoundland used by English and French ships.

2.022 _____ Most explorers were attracted by the search for the Northwest Passage and for treasure.

2.023 _____ Spain gained little or nothing from its lands in the New World.

2.024 _____ Europeans wanted to reach Asia to get cotton and opium.

80 / 100   SCORE _____   TEACHER _____ _____
                                              initials   date

3. THE FIRST COLONIES

The land claims made by all of the European nations had to be secured. The only way to do that was by establishing colonies to prove ownership by occupation. America, however, was not an easy place to live. The Europeans did not know how to raise crops there and often were too busy hunting for gold to try. The weather was harsh compared to Europe.

Disease, starvation, and attacks by hostile Native Americans decimated the settlers. In spite of the dangers, Spain, France, and England slowly established settlements. The European presence grew steadily, and the native population was pushed aside, defeated or destroyed by European diseases.

SECTION OBJECTIVES

Review these objectives. When you have completed this section, you should be able to:

4. Match Spanish, English, French, and Dutch explorers with their discoveries.
5. Describe the European colonies established in America.

VOCABULARY

Study these words to enhance your learning success in this section.

autocratic (o tu krat′ ik). A system that gives one person unlimited power.

cannibalism (kan′ u bul izm). When a person eats the flesh of another human being.

despotic (des pät′ ik). Having a ruler who exercises absolute power abusively, oppressively, or tyrannically.

dissident (dis′ u dent). A person who disagrees in opinion.

hierarchy (hī′ u rär kē). An organization of persons or things arranged into higher and lower ranks, classes or grades.

indenture (in den′ chur). To bind by contract in which a person is required to serve or work for someone else.

minority (mi nôr′ u tē). A group within a country, state or other area that is different from the larger part of the population in some way, such as race or religion.

reprisal (ri prī′ zel). An injury done in return for an injury, especially by one nation or group to another.

serf (sėrf). A peasant in the Medieval Age who was almost a slave; Serfs could not be sold off of their land, but were sold and inherited with the land.

strategic (stru tē′ jik). Useful in the planning and direction of military operations.

tenuous (ten′ yü us). Thin or slight; not substantial.

Spanish

Florida. The very first permanent European settlement in the United States was, not surprisingly, Spanish. Ironically, it began in response to an attempted French settlement. France was a Catholic nation, but it had a large **minority** of Protestants called *Huguenots*. These people were persecuted, and in 1564, a group of them began a settlement on the St. John's River in Florida. They also established Ft. Caroline located near Jacksonville in northern Florida.

The Spanish by that point had an extensive claim to Florida. Ponce de León had explored and named it in 1513. In 1521 he tried to start a settlement there. Another group, this one under Pánfilo de Narváez, came in 1528 to see how the land was connected to Mexico. Hernando de Soto had started his expedition in Florida on his way to the Mississippi River in 1539. Another attempt at colonization under Luna y Arellano was abandoned in 1561 after a hurricane. The French settlement was a threat not only to Spanish land claims, but to control of the sea lanes between Europe and the West Indies.

King Phillip II of Spain sent a force under Admiral Pedro Menéndez de Avilés to destroy the French colony. He did so in 1565, massacring the French defenders. Avilés also founded the city of St. Augustine just south of the French town. It became the first permanent European settlement in the United States.

The city was named after Augustine, an early church father on whose Feast Day Avilés spotted the Florida coast. The Spaniards built a massive masonry fort, Castillo de San Marcos, to protect the city. It had walls 30 feet (9 m) high and 12 feet (3.6 m) thick. The city served as a military headquarters for Spain in North America and was important enough for Sir Francis Drake to loot it in 1586. However, the city and the fort survived, and today the latter is a national monument.

Southwest. The Spanish also decided to occupy their land claims in the American southwest. A small settlement was established in New Mexico as early as 1598. However, in 1610

a new governor, Pedro de Peralta, founded the city of Santa Fe and made it the capital of the province. Its full name was *Villa Real de la Santa Fé de San Francisco de Asis*, the Royal city of the Holy Faith of St. Francis of Assisi. It is the oldest seat of government in the U.S.

The land in California was not occupied until much later. A military fort, Presidio, was finally established at San Diego in 1769. From that time on, Spanish Franciscan friars set up a series of missions in the state, and by 1823 they had twenty-one in California.

Spanish colonial life. The Spanish tended to be brutal conquerors. The Native Americans were enslaved to serve the Spaniards. Landowners were given large tracts of land, and they used European indentured servants, or enslaved Native American or African people. The ruler of each colony was a governor or viceroy appointed by the king, serving at his majesty's pleasure. There were no assemblies to represent local viewpoints. The system was **autocratic** and had a strict **hierarchy**. At the top were Spaniards born in Spain. Next in line were people of Spanish descent that were born in America, people of mixed Spanish and Native American heritage, and at the bottom were the Native Americans. The system did not encourage the growth of freedom. Rather it led to many bloody rebellions.

Unit 1 | **Europe Comes to America (1492–1620)**

Write true if the statement is true. If it is false, write false and change one or two words to make it true.

3.1 _____ California was the first U.S. state colonized by the Spanish.

3.2 _____ The first permanent European settlement in the United States was Santa Fe.

3.3 _____ French Protestants, called Huguenots, established a settlement in Florida.

3.4 _____ Admiral Pedro Menéndez de Avilés destroyed Fort Caroline and established St. Augustine.

3.5 _____ San Diego is the oldest seat of government in the United States.

3.6 _____ Spanish colonies were administered by a governor elected by the people.

3.7 _____ Spanish colonial rule was very autocratic.

3.8 _____ At the top of the social order in Spanish colonies were Spaniards born in America.

3.9 _____ Native American people on Spanish lands were often forced into slavery.

French and Dutch

French settlements. Most of the early French settlements were forts used as trading posts for furs. They were also established for the express purpose of blocking English and Spanish expansion into the Mississippi River basin. Most of these were built after La Salle successfully followed the course of the Mississippi in 1682. Fort Louis (present-day Ocean Springs), Mississippi was founded in 1699. Other towns include: Detroit, MI (1701); Mobile, AL (1702); Biloxi, MS (1719); New Orleans, LA (1718); and Baton Rouge, LA (1719).

French colonial life. Of the three major European countries in the U.S., the French had the best relations with the native population. This was due to two factors. First, the French were mostly interested in fur trading, and they needed the Native American people to trap for them. They were, however, quite willing to cheat the Native Americans in trade agreements. These practices were opposed by many of the Catholic priests who worked among the Native Americans. Second, the French were widely scattered over their territory. There was no large exodus from France to the New World, and the settlements grew very slowly. This made them much less of a threat to the Native Americans, and the Native Americans knew it.

There were several reasons why immigration to New France was not an attractive option for Frenchmen. The government of the colony was, as in the Spanish colonies, under the direct control of the king. Elected assemblies of the people and personal rights were unknown. The land was owned by rich landlords, and the peasant farmers on it were almost **serfs**. New France never developed a middle class of small landowner/farmers, as would be the case in the English colonies. Also, the crown tried to strictly regulate the fur trade so the king got most of the profit. These were not conditions likely to attract the kind of adventurous, independent person willing to pull up roots in Europe and try life on a new continent.

Moreover, the king's government would not allow religious freedom. Many of the colonists in English lands, as we will see, were religious **dissidents** who just wanted a place to worship in peace. The French Huguenots could have provided many willing colonists if they had been allowed to worship freely in America. Instead, these hard-working people were driven out of France, barred from New France, and often wound up in English America. Thus, the French population of New France grew with painful slowness.

Dutch settlements. Dutch land claims to the Hudson River Valley and the nearby coastlands, named New Netherlands, were developed by the Dutch West India Company. The company was organized in 1621 and given a monopoly on trade with New Netherlands by the Dutch government. Merchants had set up small trading posts in the area soon after Henry Hudson's voyage in 1609. A very profitable fur trade quickly developed, but no permanent colonization had been attempted by the time the company took control.

New Netherlands was a company colony, run as the directors saw fit. The Dutch West India Company sent thirty families over in 1624 to set up permanent bases for trade. Some of these families established Fort Orange up the Hudson River as the first successful settlement in the colony. It would later become Albany, the capital of the state of New York. Other settlements were also established along the Hudson and around the fine harbor at the river's mouth.

The most important settlement was built in the harbor on the **strategic** island of Manhattan in 1625. This island was purchased from the Native Americans by the company for the paltry sum of $24 in beads and trinkets. However, there is question about whether this story is true. The town and fort built there were named New Amsterdam. It later became New York City, one of the most important seaports in America. The Dutch colony was, however, short-lived. The English took it over in 1664.

| The St. Lawrence River

Dutch colonial life. The West India Company was concerned because too few people were settling down to stay in New Netherlands. Therefore, they made a very generous offer to its members. Members were given huge tracts of land if they could bring over fifty people to settle on it. This was called the *patroon* (landowner) system. In this way, West India merchants became the owners of great estates and the population of the colony grew at a better pace. The system set up a wealthy, privileged aristocracy in the colony and prevented small farmers from getting land for themselves.

New Netherlands was ruled by governors appointed by the West India Company. There was no religious or political freedom. The governors, also called director-generals, were interested only in profit and orderliness. The people quickly began to object to the **despotic** control of the company rulers and the patroons. Moreover, most of the governors were poor administrators. In the end, the popular discontent would aid the English in taking the colony for themselves.

Identify whether the settlement was French or Dutch.

3.10 _____ Fort Orange

3.11 _____ New Orleans

3.12 _____ Detroit

3.13 _____ New Amsterdam

3.14 _____ Mobile

Answer these questions.

3.15 What factors made New France unattractive to immigrants?

_____
_____
_____

3.16 Why did the French get along better with the Native Americans than the other Europeans?

_____
_____
_____

3.17 Who developed the Dutch claims on the Hudson River?

_____

3.18 What was the patroon system?

_____
_____
_____

3.19 Why were the people of New Netherlands unhappy?

_____
_____
_____

English

Sir Humphrey Gilbert. The English, like their European rivals, had several failures before successfully planting a colony in America. Two of the early leaders in the colonization effort were Sir Humphrey Gilbert and Sir Walter Raleigh, his half brother. Gilbert was a soldier and navigator who traveled to the Americas in 1578 in search of the Northwest Passage. He carried with him a grant from Queen Elizabeth to settle any land not already claimed by another European monarch. The world-wise Elizabeth had no interest in getting into a war over American land.

The expedition was a complete failure. The undisciplined fleet never even reached America. Gilbert tried again with seven ships in 1583. This group reached Newfoundland and claimed it for the queen. No settlements were established, and Gilbert was lost at sea on the return voyage.

Roanoke. Sir Walter Raleigh was a favorite of Queen Elizabeth and had been an active participant in his brother's plans. He sponsored a group of colonists in 1585 who settled on Roanoke Island, North Carolina. The land was named Virginia in honor of Elizabeth, the virgin queen (she never married). This first attempt was abandoned in 1586, and the settlers returned to England.

Raleigh sent another group to the island in 1587 under the command of John White. Over a hundred colonists settled on the island in July of that year. In August, Virginia Dare, John White's granddaughter, became the first English child born in America. Shortly after the birth, White returned to England for badly needed supplies. This was a time of war between Spain and England. The "Invincible Armada" attacked in 1588. It was not until August of 1590, three years later, that White was able to return.

John White found no one on the island when he arrived. There were no signs of an attack or disaster. The only possible clue was the word "Croatoan," the name of a nearby Native American tribe and their land, carved on a tree. Storms prevented the distraught father from searching the nearby lands, and he returned to England. The mystery of the Lost Colony has intrigued historians for generations. One favorite theory is that the colonists joined the Croatoans on the mainland to survive. Whatever happened, no trace of them has ever been discovered.

Raleigh was out of favor with the queen after Roanoke failed the second time. It would be seventeen years before another serious attempt was made to settle the English claims in America. By then, England had a new ruler, James I, Elizabeth's cousin. The ruler of Scotland, James united the two nations when he inherited the English throne in 1603. He granted charters to settle America in exchange for loans.

The new effort was not a personal venture like Raleigh had conducted, but a business enterprise. Two companies were given permission from the crown to settle in Virginia in 1606. The Virginia Company of London had rights to the southern half of the land, and the Virginia Company of Plymouth had rights to the north. Both were joint stock companies created by merchants to exploit the resources of the land for profit.

Jamestown. Early in 1607, a group of colonists financed by the London Company arrived in Virginia at Chesapeake Bay. The approximately one hundred surviving colonists, all men, sailed up a broad river to choose a site for settlement. They chose a spot on a peninsula that would be easy to defend against both Native Americans and Spaniards. They named the settlement Jamestown and the river the James, after their king. This was to be the first successful English settlement in America, but its success was a matter of grave doubt for many years.

The peninsula was a bad choice because it was low and marshy, subjecting the colonists to fevers from insects. The colonists themselves were not well chosen for the job of settling a wild land. Most were shiftless renegades from English society who wanted easy riches. They searched for gold rather than planting crops or building shelters. Within a year, the one hundred original settlers had been reduced to forty.

Things began to improve in 1608 when two hundred new colonists arrived and Captain John Smith took over control of the colony. Smith forced the men to work or face expulsion into the wilderness. His harsh discipline saved the colony but made him unpopular. The land was still owned by the company, and whatever a man grew was shared by all the colonists. There was little incentive for the colonists to farm, especially when the company was still pressuring them to find gold!

One of the reasons Jamestown survived was the assistance given by the Native American Peoples. The Algonquins of Virginia had a structure that many of the English settlers would encounter along the east coast. They were organized into small villages that farmed and hunted to survive. The women did the farming and the men the hunting. There was no individual ownership of land or food. Any food harvested or shot was shared. Weapons were made of stone, wood, or bone.

These Native Americans had several disadvantages with the Europeans in the upcoming battle for control of North America. The most important was their lack of unity. The various tribes were part of different Native American Nations with different customs and traditions. They fought continuously amongst each other. These wars tended to be limited to quick raids. Sustained warfare in the European style was unknown to the Native Americans. Some of the tribes quickly befriended the Europeans to gain their support in conflicts with their more traditional enemies. Unity against the newcomers was their only hope to keep their land; most failed to realize this.

The Native Americans had other disadvantages as well. Their weapons were inferior to those of the Europeans. In the beginning, they lacked gunpowder, firearms, and metal. Eventually, however, many would make up this deficit by trading with the Europeans. Another key

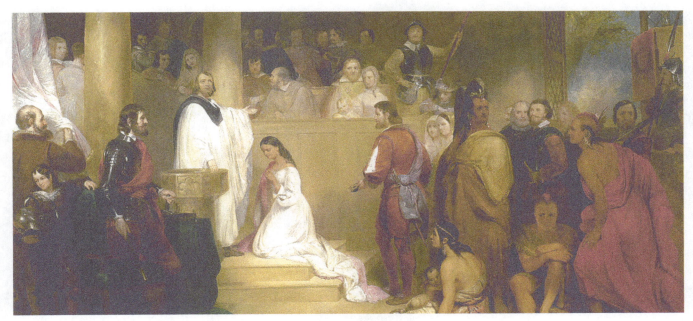

| Baptism of Pocahontas

disadvantage for the Native Americans was their lack of resistance against European diseases. It was very common for half or more of the local population to die from disease in the years after the arrival of Europeans. Smallpox, typhus, and measles were common killers. Finally, the Native Americans were just simply overwhelmed by the continuous flow of settlers. They were continuously mistreated and their lives were uprooted.

The Algonquin people of Virginia were led by Chief Powhatan who had succeeded in establishing himself as the ruler of a confederacy of several tribes. John Smith traded with the confederacy for food, or stole it when they wouldn't trade. At one point, Smith was captured by the Algonquin, and according to his account, saved from death by the chief's daughter, Pocahontas. Later the English took Pocahontas as a hostage to force the Algonquin to bring them food.

Powhatan could have destroyed Jamestown in the early years. He did not, probably because he wanted access to European goods, such as metal weapons and utensils, as well as allies. The two sides kept an uneasy peace broken by occasional raids during Powhatan's life.

 Complete these sentences.

3.20 Sir _____ and Sir _____ were half brothers who led several failed English attempts to settle America in the late 1500s.

3.21 Two different attempts were made to settle Roanoke Island in the years _____ and _____ .

3.22 _____ was the first English child born in America.

3.23 The first successful English colony in America was named for the _____ of England.

3.24 The discipline enforced by Captain _____ saved the colony at Jamestown.

3.25 The _____ people of Virginia were joined in a confederacy led by _____ .

3.26 The chief's daughter, _____ , is reported to have saved John Smith's life and was held as a hostage by the settlers to get food from the Algonquin.

Answer these questions.

3.27 What happened to the second settlement at Roanoke?

_____

_____

_____

3.28 How was the sponsorship of the settlement of Jamestown different from that at Roanoke?

_____
_____
_____

3.29 Why was the site of Jamestown chosen and why was it a bad choice?

_____
_____
_____

3.30 What were four of the disadvantages the Native Americans had in their conflict with the Europeans?

a. _____

b. _____

c. _____

d. _____

The London Company reorganized in 1609, obtained a new charter, gathered additional finances, and sent a new group of colonists to Jamestown. The success of the reorganization nearly destroyed the colony. About four hundred settlers (men, women, and children) reached Jamestown safely in August of 1609. This created a serious food and shelter problem for the colony. It was compounded by the fact that John Smith returned to England after being hurt in a gunpowder accident. The winter of 1609-1610 was called the "starving time" by the colonists. People were reduced to eating berries, plants, and acorns. There were even reports of **cannibalism**.

When Sir Thomas Gates and a shipload of settlers, who had been temporarily marooned on Bermuda, arrived in May of 1610 there were only 60 survivors. Gates decided to abandon the colony. All of the survivors were loaded onto the ship which headed down the James River. Near the Chesapeake Bay, they met Lord De La Warr bringing more settlers and supplies. He persuaded them to return and try again.

The colony survived because the new governors enforced strict discipline. The company also was able to send regular supplies and new settlers. Prosperity came on the back of what King James called "a custom loathsome to the eye, hateful to the nose, harmful to the brain (and) dangerous to the lungs,"—tobacco.

Around 1612 John Rolfe, one of the leaders of Jamestown, planted a new type of tobacco grown by the Spanish in the West Indies. Rolfe also married Pocahontas, Powhatan's daughter, in 1614. Perhaps from her Rolfe learned the Native American method of curing the harvested leaves that made the result sweeter. It quickly found a market in Europe, and Jamestown had a cash crop. For many years it would be not only the main product of the colony, but also its currency. Products would be routinely bought and sold for so many pounds of tobacco.

| Pocahontas' Wedding to John Rolfe

Pocahontas became a Christian and was baptized Rebecca after she fell in love with John Rolfe. She went with her husband to England in 1616 where she was greeted as a princess. She died of smallpox in 1617 at the age of about twenty-one. Her son, Thomas Rolfe, was educated in England and returned to Virginia to become an important settler there.

Virginia, in the meantime, began to expand beyond Jamestown. The London Company in 1618 initiated what was called the *head right*. Every settler who came to the colony and stayed 3 years was guaranteed 50 acres of his own land. Laborers who could not pay their passage to Virginia could work for seven years as **indentured** servants and then receive their land. The demand for Virginian tobacco and the promise of land to grow it encouraged more and more settlers to risk coming.

The year 1619 was a banner year for the Virginia colony. In that year, Sir George Yeardley, the colonial governor, organized an assembly to represent the colonists. This legislature was elected by all the adult men of the colony. It could only advise the governor, who was still appointed by the London Company. However, the House of Burgesses, as it was called, was the beginning of representative government in America.

That same year, the London Company sent a shipload of women over as wives for the colonists, most of whom were single men. The women quickly found spouses, who had to pay the company 120 pounds of tobacco for each wife's passage. Later, groups of women were equally welcome and quickly married. Virginia now took on a more permanent air as families and farms were established.

Also in 1619, the first enslaved Africans arrived in Jamestown. A Dutch ship traded twenty black laborers for supplies on a stop at the settlement. They were sold as indentured servants. Later, the term of servitude for black people would be for life, since the colony began to desperately need workers for the tobacco fields.

The success of the colony found another threat as relations with nearby Native Americans changed. Pocahontas died in 1617 and Powhatan, her father, died the following year, removing two important influences for peace between the two peoples. The new chief, Opechancanough, was rightly concerned by the continued influx of English settlers. Native American hunting and farming lands were being taken over by the English. The settlers also showed little respect for the natives, and violent incidents were common.

Opechancanough decided to drive the English out completely. He organized an alliance among the tribes of the area, and they attacked without warning on Good Friday 1622. Approximately three hundred and fifty colonists were killed. However, the over one thousand survivors were able to defeat the Native Americans and counter with fierce **reprisals**.

The Native American attack was the last straw for the London Company. It had gone deeply into debt supporting the colony. The king revoked its charter in 1624, and the company eventually went bankrupt. Virginia became a "crown colony" ruled directly by the king, although it was allowed to maintain the House of Burgesses.

Under the leadership of the now elderly Opechancanough, the Algonquins tried again to destroy the colony in 1644. Almost 500 colonists died in that attack. It was no use, as the colony was over 8,000 strong by then. The governor, Sir William Berkeley, led a spirited counterattack that broke the power of the united Native American groups in Virginia and captured the old chief. Thereafter, the Native Americans were confined to reservation lands that often were not protected from later settlers. The attacks also convinced the settlers that Native Americans were 'dangerous savages'. That negative view of Native Americans would continue throughout the settlement of the entire country.

Conclusion. As you will study in the next LIFEPAC, the English continued to establish colonies along the eastern coast of North America. They also took over the Dutch colony in what is now New York. By the early 1700s, there were only three major contenders for North America: England, France, and Spain. These three nations were rivals in Europe as well as America. In the century that followed, the wars of Europe would grow to include battle for control of North America.

Spain had been the first power to reach the continent, but north of Mexico its hold was **tenuous**. The Spanish government was mainly interested in the precious metals of Mexico and South America. Little effort had been taken to secure the northern claims. Colonists in Spanish lands were few and formed the top of an autocratic pyramid. The Spanish people born in the New World were ranked lower than those born in Spain. That limited the loyalty of the new Spanish Americans. Spain, however, was still a major power in 1700, and its claims could not be lightly ignored by France and England.

France had a huge claim over the heartland of the United States in 1700. France was England's greatest rival through that century. The French lands were not heavily populated, and New France did not attract many settlers. The autocratic organization allowed the government to act quickly to defend French claims. Those claims were the most dangerous to the English settlers because they blocked the new colonies from expanding westward.

It was the English who eventually won the northern continent, but in 1700 that was not an obvious outcome. The presence of two powerful rivals and the many Native American Nations cast grave doubts on the success of the English colonies. Despite this, England was poised to build itself into the greatest power on earth, and it would gather up North America on the way. It would also unwittingly establish thriving, freedom-loving colonies that would challenge that power.

Answer these questions.

3.31 Why did the successful reorganization of the London Company in 1609 almost destroy Jamestown?
_____
_____
_____

3.32 What was the head right?
_____
_____
_____

3.33 What three key things happened in Virginia in 1619?

a. _____

b. _____

c. _____

3.34 What were the results of the Native American attack of 1622?
_____
_____
_____

3.35 What were the results of the Native American attack of 1644?
_____
_____
_____

3.36 What product provided Virginia with a cash crop? _____

3.37 What is the difference between an indentured servant and a slave? (Use outside references if you need them.)
_____
_____
_____

3.38 Who was the famous wife of John Rolfe? _____

3.39 By about 1700, who were the three main European rivals in North America and what land did each claim?

a. _____
_____
_____

b. _____
_____
_____

c. _____
_____
_____

Before you take this last Self Test, you may want to do one or more of these self checks.

1. _____ Read the objectives. See if you can do them.
2. _____ Restudy the material related to any objectives that you cannot do.
3. _____ Use the **SQ3R** study procedure to review the material:
   a. **S**can the sections.
   b. **Q**uestion yourself.
   c. **R**ead to answer your questions.
   d. **R**ecite the answers to yourself.
   e. **R**eview areas you did not understand.
4. _____ Review all vocabulary, activities, and Self Tests, writing a correct answer for every wrong answer.

SELF TEST 3

Name the European country that established each colony (each answer, 2 points).

3.01 _____ Fort Orange
3.02 _____ Jamestown
3.03 _____ New Orleans
3.04 _____ St. Augustine
3.05 _____ New Amsterdam
3.06 _____ Quebec
3.07 _____ Roanoke
3.08 _____ San Diego
3.09 _____ Santa Fe
3.010 _____ Detroit

Match these items (each answer, 2 points).

3.011 _____ John Smith
3.012 _____ Ponce de León
3.013 _____ Marco Polo
3.014 _____ Henry the Navigator
3.015 _____ Leif Ericson
3.016 _____ Magellan
3.017 _____ Sir Francis Drake
3.018 _____ John Cabot
3.019 _____ Henry Hudson
3.020 _____ Champlain

a. led first European attempt to colonize America
b. explored the coast of New York, north Canada for England and Netherlands
c. Leader of the first English colony whose strict discipline saved it
d. led the first successful circumnavigation of the world, did not complete it himself
e. sea dog, circumnavigated the world attacking Spanish ports
f. explored and named Florida while searching for the fountain of youth
g. visited China in the 1200s and wrote a best selling book about it
h. Father of New France, established first French colony in Canada
i. organized Portuguese voyages around Africa to the Far East
j. explored Canada and found the Grand Banks for England shortly after Columbus

Write France, England, or Spain for each statement (each answer, 3 points).

3.021 _____ by 1700 claimed most of the central United States from the Appalachians to the Rockies

3.022 _____ James I gave charters to two joint stock companies to settle Virginia

3.023 _____ controlled Florida and much of the southwest United States by 1700

3.024 _____ Huguenots were driven out of the country and barred from the colonies

3.025 _____ set up the first successful European settlement in the United States

3.026 _____ were interested primarily in the fur trade

3.027 _____ enslaved the Native Americans

3.028 _____ had the best relations of the three with the Native Americans

3.029 _____ much of the exploration was by *coureurs de bois* who set up trading posts

3.030 _____ Sir Humphrey Gilbert and Sir Walter Raleigh sponsored early failures

Check the statements that are true of Jamestown (each answer, 2 points).

3.031 _____ It was the second successful English colony in America.

3.032 _____ The location was bad because it was swampy and unhealthy.

3.033 _____ The local Algonquin People fought against the colonists continuously from the time they first arrived.

3.034 _____ The colony prospered when cotton was established as a cash crop.

3.035 _____ The House of Burgesses was an elected assembly organized for the colony in 1619.

3.036 _____ The Algonquins were not able to destroy the colony, but they did drive the London Company into bankruptcy.

3.037 _____ The starving time in the winter of 1609-1610 came about because of the sudden arrival of a large number of colonists when there was not enough food for them.

3.038 _____ The head right gave every male colonist the right to vote.

3.039 _____ The first colonists were more interested in searching for gold than planting crops or building shelters.

3.040 _____ The colony was nearly abandoned after the starving time left only sixty survivors.

Answer these questions (each answer, 2 points).

3.041 What are two of the disadvantages Native Americans had in the battle with Europeans for control of North America?

a. _____

b. _____

3.042 What was the *patroon* system in the Dutch colony?

_____

_____

3.043 Dutch claims were primarily along what river?

_____

3.044 What are two reasons New France was unattractive to settlers?

a. _____

b. _____

Before taking the LIFEPAC Test, you may want to do one or more of these self checks.

1. _____ Read the objectives. See if you can do them.
2. _____ Restudy the material related to any objectives that you cannot do.
3. _____ Use the **SQ3R** study procedure to review the material.
4. _____ Review activities, Self Tests, and LIFEPAC vocabulary words.
5. _____ Restudy areas of weakness indicated by the last Self Test.

Unit 801 | **History & Geography**

HISTORY & GEOGRAPHY 801

LIFEPAC TEST

NAME _____

DATE _____

SCORE _____

HISTORY & GEOGRAPHY 801: LIFEPAC TEST

Match these items (each answer, 2 points).

1. _____ Polo
2. _____ Da Gama
3. _____ Columbus
4. _____ Balboa
5. _____ Magellan
6. _____ Cortes
7. _____ Pizarro
8. _____ Ponce de León
9. _____ Coronado
10. _____ De Soto
11. _____ Cabot
12. _____ Drake
13. _____ Hudson
14. _____ Cartier
15. _____ Champlain
16. _____ Jolliet
17. _____ John Smith
18. _____ La Salle
19. _____ Raleigh
20. _____ Leif Ericson

a. first to see the Pacific Ocean
b. began the first permanent French colony
c. sponsored the Lost Colony at Roanoke
d. lived in China for twenty years
e. conquered the Incas of Peru
f. discovered fishing grounds off Newfoundland
g. first to explore the St. Lawrence River
h. led first European settlement attempt
i. first to sail around the world
j. followed the Mississippi to the Gulf
k. conquered the Aztecs of Mexico
l. explored the North American southwest
m. claimed the area of New York for Dutch
n. discovered the Mississippi River
o. explored the Mississippi with Marquette
p. disciplined leader of Jamestown
q. searched for the Fountain of Youth
r. discovered the New World
s. looted Spanish vessels for England
t. sailed around Africa to India

Write the correct letter in the blank (each answer, 2 points).

21. In the early exploration of North America, all of the following rivers were important *except* _____ .
    a. St. Lawrence   b. Hudson   c. Mississippi   d. Columbia

22. The nations to claim land in North America included all but _____ .
    a. Spain   b. Portugal   c. Netherlands   d. France

23. Old World events which sparked exploration included all but _____ .
    a. the Crusades
    b. Polo's journeys
    c. the power of the Roman Empire
    d. the difficulty of land trade with China

24. Columbus explored all the following *except* _____ .
    a. South America   b. Central America   c. Caribbean Islands   d. Canada

25. The explorers who tried to find a passage to the East around the Americas included all but _____ .
    a. Magellan   b. Hudson   c. Drake   d. Cortes

26. Successful New World colonies were started by all *except* _____ .
    a. Columbus
    b. Raleigh
    c. Dutch West India Co.
    d. Champlain

27. Spanish and French colonies shared all these characteristics *except* _____ .
    a. autocratic governments
    b. no freedom of religion
    c. enslaved the Native Americans
    d. large pieces of land were owned by wealthy landlords

28. All of the following are roots of Western Civilization *except* _____ .
    a. Roman Empire
    b. Greek civilization
    c. Anglo-Saxon civilization
    d. Christianity

29. The disadvantages that the Native Americans had in stopping the European takeover of their lands included all of the following *except* _____ .
    a. no immunity against European diseases
    b. a cultural history that denounced fighting
    c. lack of metal and firearms
    d. lack of unity between the tribes

30. Columbus failed in all of the following ways *except* _____ .
    a. he did not discover a route to Asia
    b. the lands he discovered had no value for Spain
    c. he was not able to control the lands he found
    d. the land he discovered was not named after him

Name the item or person being described (each answer, 3 points).

31. _____ cash crop of Virginia

32. _____ country that signed the Treaty of Tordesillas with Spain to divide the non-Catholic world into two parts

33. _____ Portuguese prince who organized voyages around Africa

34. _____ country whose cities held a monopoly on the Asian trade before the 1490s

35. _____ English pirates and privateers who attacked Spanish shipping under Elizabeth I of England

36. _____ many American explorers were searching for this passage around America and never found it

37. _____ rich fishing grounds off Canada visited by European fishermen for years before permanent settlements

38. _____ French Protestants

39. _____ main trade item for the French and Dutch in North America

40. _____ first permanent European settlement in the United States

Write true or false in the blank (each answer, 1 point).

41. _____ Most of the culture of America came from Europe.

42. _____ Jamestown was a stable, well run colony from its beginning.

43. _____ Jamestown was created as a royal colony under King James I.

44. _____ French lands in America were not heavily populated.

45. _____ The House of Burgesses was the beginning of representative government in America.

46. _____ Spain went into decline by the end of the 1500s and was not able to stop other countries from colonizing the New World.

47. _____ Columbus underestimated the size of the earth and thought Asia went further east than it really does.

48. _____ Columbus realized by the time of his death that he had not reached Asia.

49. _____ The Dutch were a significant rival of England for control of North America in the 1700s.

50. _____ Champlain made the Iroquois faithful French allies after he explored their region.